Budget Buster

FAMILY
COOKBOOK
FEED FOUR OR MORE FOR

$10 OR
LESS!

This edition published in 2009

Love Food ® is an imprint of Parragon Books Ltd

Parragon Publishing
Queen Street House
4 Queen Street
Bath BA1 1HE, UK

Internal design by Fiona Roberts.
Photography and text by The Bridgewater Book Company Ltd.

ISBN: 978-1-4075-7740-1

Printed in China

NOTE
Cup measurements in this book are for American cups. This book also uses imperial and
metric measurements. Follow the same units of measurement throughout; do not mix
imperial and metric. All spoon measurements are level: teaspoons are assumed to be 5 ml
and tablespoons are assumed to be 15 ml. Unless otherwise stated, milk is assumed to be
whole milk, eggs and individual vegetables such as potatoes are medium, and pepper is
freshly ground black pepper.

The times given for each recipe are an approximate guide only because the preparation times
may differ according to the techniques used by different people and the cooking times may
vary as a result of the type of oven used.

Recipes using raw or very lightly cooked eggs should be avoided by infants, the elderly,
pregnant women, convalescents, and anyone with a chronic condition.

contents

introduction

Our mothers and grandmothers, who often raised larger families than those of today, knew a thing or two about how to prepare tasty, wholesome, and filling meals on a tight budget. Nowadays we are pressured not only by a shortage of time, but also by advertising, so it is all too easy to resort to ready-made products. This is an expensive way to feed a family and is nothing like so delicious or healthy as home-cooked meals.

Fresh is not just best, it is more flavorsome and nutritious and it doesn't have to be expensive. When buying fruit and vegetables think seasonal. Strawberries in the midwinter might seem like a treat, but they are often disappointingly tasteless and absurdly priced, whereas home-grown apples are in season, delicious, and inexpensive. The less expensive cuts of meat, such as braising steak, are often the ones with most flavor—they just require longer, slower cooking, but this results in tender and succulent casseroles, stews, and curries. What's more, these kinds of dishes are incredibly easy to prepare.

Shopping

Plan the week's menus before you go shopping, write a list, and stick to it. Bear in mind that supermarkets take great care to display their products to tempt customers to buy more than they need and to choose the more expensive brands. You may not be aware that to reach staples, such as flour, rice, and pasta, you will have to push your cart past eye-catching shelves stacked with colorfully packaged cookies, potato chips, and jars of ready-made sauces. The more expensive brands are usually displayed on shelves at eye level, while the cheaper varieties are placed lower down.

There are bargains to be had, but think twice before you put the "two for the price of one" or "15 per cent extra" bag in your basket. Check the "use-by" date as it's no bargain if you end up throwing half of it away. Nor is it value for money if it's not something the family is going to like. Nevertheless, such special offers can extend the budget if they apply to things you know you will use, especially if you can store them in the freezer.

Money-saving tips

■ Allow plenty of time for shopping rather than having to make a harassed dash around the supermarket on a Friday evening and, if you can, leave the kids at home.

BUDGETING GUIDE	
$	Bargain
$$	Budget
$$$	Economical

■ Don't go shopping on an empty stomach as you are more likely to be tempted to buy things you don't really need.

■ If you are going to heat up the oven for one dish, save energy and therefore money by adding

There are hundreds of dishes to make using the simplest of ingredients

another—a main course casserole and a pie for dessert. Cook ahead for tomorrow while cooking tonight's dinner or bake in batches.

■ Steaming is a great way to cook greens and you can save energy by cooking one thing on top of another.

■ If a recipe requires chicken portions, buy a whole chicken and cut it into pieces with a heavy knife or cleaver.

■ Fresh herbs are fabulous for adding flavor to all kinds of dishes and are much

Fabulous family meals can be created
without great expense

less expensive than ready-made sauces. If you can grow them in your yard, in a

window-box, or in pots the kitchen, they are virtually free and truly fresh.

■ Make your own stock and freeze it in ice cube trays—it keeps for up to six

months. You can add one or two cubes whenever stock is required and this is

much cheaper, tastier, and probably healthier than using bouillon powder or cubes.

■ Save the carcasses and bones from roast chicken for making stock. Store them

in a plastic bag in the freezer until you have enough for the recipe (see page 9).

■ Peel potatoes after boiling them (scrub them first). Not only will there be

less waste, but more vitamins will be retained.

■ Make the most of cheap-and-cheerful fillers, such as pasta, rice, potatoes,

legumes, pastry, and dumplings.

old-fashioned chicken stock

- makes 2.5 litres/4½ pints
- prepared in 16 minutes, plus chilling
- cooks in 3¼ hours

2 tbsp vegetable oil

2 lb 12 oz chicken and/or turkey
   wings, necks, and backs or 4
   carcasses and bones from
   whole roast chickens

2 onions, cut into fourths

2 celery stalks, coarsely chopped

2 carrots, coarsely chopped

4 fresh parsley sprigs

2 fresh thyme sprigs

1 bay leaf

8 black peppercorns, coarsely
   crushed

1 Heat the oil in a large pan and cook the chicken or turkey and onions over medium heat, stirring and turning occasionally, for 10 - 15 minutes until lightly browned.

2 Pour in 17½ cups (8½ pints) water and stir well, scraping up any sediment from the base of the pan. Bring to a boil and skim off any scum that rises to the surface. Add all the remaining ingredients, lower the heat, cover, and simmer for 3 hours.

3 Strain the stock into a bowl, let cool, then chill in the refrigerator. When the stock is cold, remove the layer of fat that has formed on the surface.

soups, snacks & sides

Serve the delicious dishes in this chapter as appetizers and light

meals or as filling accompaniments without breaking the bank.

Homemade soup is always a welcome treat, while other favorites

include Potato Omelet, Potato Frittata, Vegetarian Chili,

and Vegetable Pancakes.

$$

tomato soup

- serves 4
- prepared in 10 mins
- cooks in 25 mins

2 oz/55 g butter

1 onion, finely chopped

**1 lb 9 oz/700 g tomatoes,
finely chopped**

salt and pepper

**2½ cups hot chicken or vegetable
stock**

pinch of sugar

generous ⅓ cup light cream

2 tbsp shredded fresh basil leaves

1 tbsp chopped fresh parsley

1 Melt half the butter in a large, heavy-bottom pan. Add the onion and cook over low heat, stirring occasionally, for 5 minutes, or until softened. Add the tomatoes, season to taste with salt and pepper, and cook for 5 minutes.

2 Pour in the hot chicken stock, return to a boil, then reduce the heat, and cook for 10 minutes.

3 Push the soup through a strainer with the back of a wooden spoon to remove the tomato skins and seeds. Return to the pan and stir in the sugar, cream, remaining butter, basil, and parsley. Heat through briefly, but do not let boil. Ladle into warmed soup bowls and serve immediately.

1 2 3

cream of chicken soup

 $$$

- serves 4
- prepared in 15 mins + 10 mins to cool
- cooks in 40 mins

3 tbsp butter

4 shallots, chopped

1 leek, trimmed and sliced

1 lb/450 g skinless chicken
breasts, chopped

2½ cups chicken bouillon

1 tbsp chopped fresh parsley

1 tbsp chopped fresh thyme

salt and pepper

¾ cup heavy cream

sprigs of fresh thyme,
to garnish

fresh crusty rolls, to serve

1 Melt the butter in a large pan over medium heat. Add the shallots and cook, stirring, for 3 minutes, until slightly softened. Add the leek and cook for another 5 minutes, stirring. Add the chicken, bouillon, and herbs, and season with salt and pepper. Bring to a boil, then lower the heat and simmer for 25 minutes, until the chicken is tender and cooked through. Remove from the heat and let cool for 10 minutes.

2 Transfer the soup into a food processor and blend until smooth (you may need to do this in batches). Return the soup to the pan and warm over low heat for 5 minutes.

3 Stir in the cream and cook for another 2 minutes, then remove from the heat and ladle into serving bowls. Garnish with sprigs of thyme and serve with fresh crusty rolls.

vegetable chowder

$$

- serves 4
- prepared in 15 mins
- cooks in 45 mins

2 tbsp butter

1 large onion, finely chopped

1 large leek, split lengthwise
and thinly sliced

1–2 garlic cloves, crushed

6 tbsp all-purpose flour

5 cups vegetable bouillon

3 carrots, finely diced

2 stalks celery, finely diced

1 turnip, finely diced

1 large potato, finely diced

3–4 sprigs fresh thyme, or ⅛ tsp
dried thyme

1 bay leaf

1½ cups light cream

2¼ cups grated sharp
Cheddar cheese

salt and pepper

sprig of fresh thyme,
to garnish

1 Melt the butter in a large, heavy pan over medium-low heat. Add the onion, leek, and garlic. Cover and cook for about 5 minutes, stirring frequently, until the vegetables start to soften.

2 Stir the flour into the vegetables and continue cooking for 2 minutes. Add a little of the bouillon and stir well, scraping the bottom of the pan to mix in the flour. Bring to a boil, stirring frequently, and slowly stir in the rest of the bouillon.

3 Add the carrots, celery, turnip, potato, thyme, and bay leaf. Reduce the heat, cover, and cook gently for about 35 minutes, stirring occasionally, until the vegetables are tender. Remove the bay leaf and the thyme sprigs.

4 Stir the light cream into the soup and simmer over very low heat for 5 minutes. Add the grated cheese a handful at a time, stirring constantly for 1 minute after each addition, to make sure it is completely melted.

5 Taste the soup and adjust the seasoning, adding salt if needed, and pepper to taste.

6 Serve immediately in warm bowls, garnished with a sprig of fresh thyme.

2   3   4

carrot soup

- serves 4 - 6
- prepared in 15 mins
- cooks in 45 mins

3 tbsp butter or margarine	2 tsp tomato paste
1 large onion, chopped	2 tsp lemon juice
1–2 garlic cloves, crushed	2 fresh or dried bay leaves
3 cups carrots, sliced	about 1¼ cups skim milk
3 ¾ cups vegetable bouillon	salt and pepper
¾ tsp ground cumin	celery leaves, to garnish
2 celery stalks, thinly sliced	
1 cup potato, diced	

1 Melt the butter or margarine in a large pan. Add the onion and garlic and cook very gently until soft.

2 Add the carrots and cook gently for a further 5 minutes, stirring frequently and taking care they do not brown.

3 Add the bouillon, cumin, seasoning, celery, potato, tomato paste, lemon juice, and bay leaves and bring to a boil. Cover and simmer for about 30 minutes until the vegetables are tender.

2

4 Remove and discard the bay leaves, cool the soup a little, and then press it through a strainer or process in a food processor or blender until smooth.

5 Pour the soup into a clean pan, add the milk, and bring to a boil over low heat. Taste and adjust the seasoning if necessary.

4

6 Ladle into warmed bowls, garnish each serving with a small celery leaf and serve.

5

pea & ham soup

$$

- serves 4
- prepared in 10 mins + 10 mins to cool
- cooks in 45 mins

1 tbsp butter
1 onion, sliced
1 leek, trimmed and sliced
4 cups vegetable bouillon
1 lb/450 g freshly shelled
  peas, or frozen peas,
  thawed

7 oz/200 g lean smoked
  ham, chopped
1 bay leaf
1 tbsp chopped fresh
  tarragon
salt and pepper
4 tbsp heavy cream
cooked ham, chopped

sprigs of fresh tarragon,
  to garnish
fresh crusty rolls, to serve

1 Melt the butter in a large pan over medium heat. Add the onion and cook, stirring, for 3 minutes, until slightly softened. Add the leek and cook for another 2 minutes, stirring. Stir in the bouillon, then add the peas, ham, bay leaf, and tarragon. Season with salt and pepper. Bring to a boil, then lower the heat and simmer for 30 minutes. Remove from the heat and discard the bay leaf. Let cool for 10 minutes.

2 Transfer half of the soup into a food processor and blend until smooth. Return to the pan with the rest of the soup, stir in the cream, and cook over low heat for another 5 minutes.

3 Remove the soup from the heat and ladle into serving bowls. Garnish with chopped ham and sprigs of fresh tarragon and serve with fresh crusty rolls.

potato au gratin

- serves 4
- prepared in 25 mins
- cooks in 30 mins

2 lb/900 g mealy potatoes, diced

2 tbsp butter

2 tbsp milk

½ cup grated sharp cheese or
   blue cheese

CRISP TOPPING

3 tbsp butter

1 onion, cut into chunks

1 garlic clove, crushed

1 tbsp wholegrain mustard

3 cups fresh whole-wheat bread
   crumbs

2 tbsp chopped fresh parsley

salt and pepper

1 Cook the potatoes in a pan of lightly salted boiling water for 10 minutes or until cooked through.

2 Meanwhile, make the crisp topping. Melt the butter in a skillet. Add the onion, garlic, and wholegrain mustard and cook gently for 5 minutes, stirring constantly, until the onion chunks have softened.

3 Put the bread crumbs and parsley in a mixing bowl and stir in the onion. Season to taste with salt and pepper.

4 Drain the potatoes thoroughly and place them in a mixing bowl. Add the butter and milk, then mash until smooth. Stir in the grated cheese while the potato is still hot.

5 Spoon the mashed potato into a shallow casserole and sprinkle with the crisp topping.

6 Cook in a preheated oven, 400°F/200°C, for 10–15 minutes until the crisp topping is golden brown and crunchy. Serve immediately.

2   4   5

tomato and onion casserole

$

- serves 4
- prepared in 10 mins
- cooks in 1 hour

4 tbsp butter, plus extra for greasing
2 large onions, thinly sliced
1 lb/450 g tomatoes, skinned and sliced
2 cups fresh white bread crumbs
4 eggs
salt and ground black pepper

1 Grease an ovenproof dish with butter. Melt 3 tablespoons of the butter in a heavy skillet. Add the onions and cook over low heat, stirring occasionally, for 5 minutes, until soft.

2

2 Layer the onions, tomatoes, and bread crumbs in the dish, seasoning each layer with salt and pepper to taste. Dot the remaining butter on top and bake in a preheated oven, 350°F/180°C, for 40 minutes.

2

3 Make 4 hollows in the mixture with the back of a spoon. Crack 1 egg into each hollow. Return the dish to the oven and bake for 15 minutes more, until the eggs are just set. Serve immediately.

3

potato omelet

$

- serves 6
- prepared in 20 mins
- cooks in 35 mins

½ cup olive oil
1½ lb/675 g potatoes, sliced
1 large onion, sliced
1 large garlic clove, crushed
6 large eggs
salt and pepper

1 Heat a 10 inch skillet, preferably non-stick, over high heat. Pour in the oil and heat. Lower the heat, add the potatoes, onion, and garlic and cook for 15–20 minutes, stirring frequently, until the potatoes are tender.

2 Beat the eggs together in a large bowl and season generously with salt and pepper. Using a slotted spoon, transfer the potatoes and onion to the bowl of eggs. Pour the excess oil left in the skillet into a heatproof pitcher, then scrape off the crusty bits from the base of the pan.

3 Reheat the skillet. Add about 2 tablespoons of the oil reserved in the pitcher. Pour in the potato mixture, smoothing the vegetables into an even layer. Cook for about 5 minutes, shaking the skillet occasionally, or until the base of the omelet is set.

4 Shake the pan and use a spatula to loosen the side of the omelet. Place a large plate face down over the pan. Carefully invert the omelet onto the plate.

5 If you are not using a nonstick skillet, add 1 tablespoon of the reserved oil to the skillet and swirl around. Gently slide the omelet back into the skillet, cooked-side up. Use the spatula to "tuck down" the edge. Continue cooking over medium heat for 3–5 minutes until set.

6 Remove the skillet from the heat and slide the omelet onto a serving plate. Let it cool for at least 5 minutes before cutting. Serve hot, warm, or at room temperature with salad.

1   3

4

$$

cheese & potato slices

- serves 4
- prepared in 10 mins
- cooks in 40 mins

2 lb/900 g large waxy
  potatoes, unpeeled
  and thickly sliced
1 cup fresh white bread
  crumbs
½ cup grated Parmesan
  cheese
1½ tsp chili powder

2 eggs, beaten
oil, for deep frying
chili powder, for optional

1 Cook the sliced potatoes in a pan of boiling water for about 10–15 minutes, or until they are just tender. Drain thoroughly.

2 Mix the bread crumbs, cheese, and chili powder together in a bowl, then transfer to a shallow dish. Pour the beaten eggs into a separate shallow dish.

3 Dip the potato slices first in egg and then roll them in the bread crumbs to coat completely.

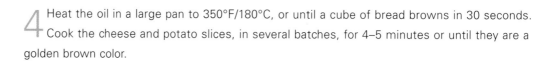

4 Heat the oil in a large pan to 350°F/180°C, or until a cube of bread browns in 30 seconds. Cook the cheese and potato slices, in several batches, for 4–5 minutes or until they are a golden brown color.

5 Remove the cheese and potato slices from the oil with a slotted spoon and drain thoroughly on paper towels. Keep the cheese and potato slices warm while you cook the remaining batches.

6 Transfer the cheese and potato slices to warm individual serving plates. Dust lightly with chili powder, if using, and serve immediately.

NOTE: If you invest in a block of fresh Parmesan it can be stored in the fridge for a long period and thus becomes an economical ingredient.

pan-fried liver and potato pancakes

$$

- serves 4
- prepared in 20 mins
- cooks in 20 - 30 mins

1 lb/450 g potatoes, peeled
1 egg, beaten
4 tbsp all-purpose white
   flour, plus extra for dusting
salt and pepper
1 lb/450 g sliced lamb's liver
sunflower oil, for frying
4 bacon strips
2 onions, sliced thinly

1 Grate the potatoes, then rinse under cold running water until the water runs clear. Squeeze out the water and dry the potatoes in a clean dish towel. Put the potatoes in a large bowl and add the egg, flour, salt, and pepper and mix well together. Dust the liver with flour and add salt and pepper.

2 Heat about ¼ inch/5 mm oil in a large skillet, then add large tablespoons of the potato mixture, flattening them with a spatula. Cook for about 10 minutes, turning once, until golden brown. Remove from the skillet and keep hot. Continue until all the mixture has been cooked.

3 In a separate skillet, heat enough oil to cover the bottom. Add the bacon and cook until crisp, then push to one side. Add the onions and cook for 5 minutes, or until browned. Push to one side of the skillet, add the liver, and cook for 6–8 minutes, turning once, until tender. Serve with the potato cakes.

2

potato frittata

$

- serves 4
- prepared in 15 mins
- cooks in 1 hour

1 lb/450 g potatoes, unpeeled
generous ¼ cup butter
salt and pepper
8 oz/225 g cabbage
2–3 tbsp water
4 tbsp corn oil
1 onion, finely chopped

1 Cook the potatoes in lightly salted boiling water for 25 minutes, or until tender. Drain and peel, then cut them into dice. Place the potatoes in a large bowl with all but 2 teaspoons of the butter and mash until no lumps remain. Season to taste with salt and pepper. Meanwhile, shred the cabbage, place it in a large, heavy-bottomed pan, and add the remaining butter and the water. Cover and cook over low heat, shaking the pan occasionally, for 10 minutes, or until tender.

2 Mix the cabbage and mashed potato together in a bowl and season to taste with salt and pepper. Heat half the oil in a heavy-bottomed skillet. Add the onion and cook, stirring occasionally, for 5 minutes, or until softened. Add the potato and cabbage mixture and press down with the back of a wooden spoon to make a flat, even cake.

3 Cook over medium heat for 15 minutes, until the underside is golden brown. Invert the vegetable cake on to a large plate. Add the remaining oil to the skillet. Return the cake to the skillet to cook the other side. Cook for 10 minutes, or until the second side is golden brown. Transfer to a plate, cut into wedges, and serve.

1   1   2

cheese casserole

$

- serves 4
- prepared in 30 mins
- cooks in 45 mins

¼ cup butter or margarine

1 bunch scallions, sliced

6 slices of white or whole-wheat bread, crusts removed

1½ cups sharp Cheddar cheese, grated

2 eggs

scant 2 cups milk

salt and pepper

flat-leaf parsley sprigs, to garnish

1 Lightly grease a 2½ pint/1.5 liter ovenproof dish with a little of the butter or margarine.

2 Melt the remaining butter or margarine in a small pan. Add the scallions and cook over medium heat, stirring occasionally, until soft and golden.

3

3 Meanwhile, cut the bread into triangles and place half of them in the base of the dish. Cover with the sliced scallions and top with half the grated Cheddar cheese.

4 Beat together the eggs and milk and season to taste with salt and pepper. Layer the remaining triangles of bread in the dish and carefully pour over the milk mixture. Let soak for 15–20 minutes.

4

5 Sprinkle the remaining cheese over the soaked bread. Bake in a preheated oven, 375°F/190°C, for 35–40 minutes, until puffed up and golden brown.

6 Garnish with flat-leaf parsley and serve immediately.

5

vegetarian chili

$

- serves 4 - 6
- prepared in 10 mins + 8 hrs soaking
- cooks in 1 hr 20 mins

7 oz/200 g dried mixed beans,
   such as kidney, soy, pinto,
   cannellini, and chickpeas
1 red onion, diced
1 garlic clove, crushed
1 tbsp hot chili powder
14 oz/400 g canned chopped
   tomatoes in tomato juice
1 tbsp tomato paste
4 tbsp lowfat plain yogurt
baked potatoes, boiled rice,
   or soft flour tortilla wraps,
   to serve

1 Soak the beans overnight or for 8 hours in a large bowl of cold water. Drain, rinse, and put the beans into a large pan. Cover well with cold water, then bring to a boil and boil rapidly for 10 minutes. Reduce the heat, cover, and let simmer for an additional 45 minutes, or until tender. Drain. (Alternatively, if time is short, use 1 lb/450 g drained and rinsed canned mixed beans and start at Step 2.)

2 Put the cooked beans, onion, garlic, chili powder, tomatoes, and tomato paste into a pan and bring to a boil. Reduce the heat, cover, and let simmer for 20–25 minutes, or until the onion is tender.

3 Serve each portion of the chili with a tablespoon of the yogurt, accompanied by baked potatoes, boiled rice, or soft flour tortilla wraps.

1   2   2

baked potato

- serves 4
- prepared in 15 mins
- cooks in 1 hour 10 mins

4 baking potatoes
½ cup vegetable bouillon
1 onion, finely chopped
1 garlic clove, finely chopped
½ cup unsweetened yogurt
2 tsp paprika
salt and ground black pepper

1

1 Prick the potatoes with a fork and bake in a preheated oven, 400°F/ 200°C , for about 1 hour, until tender.

2 Just before the potatoes are ready, pour the bouillon into a pan and add the onion and garlic. Bring to a boil and simmer for 5 minutes.

3 Remove the potatoes from the oven and cut a lengthwise slice from the top of each. Do not switch off the oven. Using a teaspoon, carefully scoop out the flesh, leaving a shell. Stir the potato flesh into the onion mixture, then add half the yogurt and 1½ teaspoons of the paprika and season to taste with salt and pepper. Mix well and push through a strainer with the back of a wooden spoon.

3

4 Spoon the potato mixture into the potato shells and return to the oven for 10 minutes, until heated through. Top the potatoes with the remaining yogurt, sprinkle the remaining paprika over it, and serve immediately.

4

vegetable pancakes

$

- serves 4
- prepared in 10 mins
- cooks in 20 mins

2 large waxy potatoes
2 medium zucchini
1 egg, beaten
2 cups fresh bread crumbs
salt and pepper
oil for shallow frying

1 Peel and grate the potatoes. Turn into a strainer and drain out all the water and starch, pressing down hard.

2 Trim the zucchini and grate into a large bowl.

2

3 Combine the grated potatoes with the zucchini. Mix the egg and bread crumbs into the vegetables and season with salt and pepper to taste.

3

4 Heat the oil in a large skillet. Drop spoonfuls of the vegetable mixture into the hot oil and press down gently to make pancakes.

5 Fry the pancakes over high heat for 5–10 minutes (depending on their thickness), until the bottom is golden brown and crispy. Turn and cook until the second side is brown and crispy. Lift out gently, drain on paper towels, place on a serving dish, and keep warm until all the pancakes are cooked. Serve immediately.

3

potato & onion bake

$

- serves 4
- prepared in 10 mins
- cooks in 50 mins

900 g/2 lb waxy potatoes, cut
   into cubes
4½ oz/125 g/½ cup butter
1 red onion, cut into 8
2 garlic cloves, crushed
1 tsp lemon juice
2 tbsp chopped thyme
salt and pepper

1 Cook the cubed potatoes in a saucepan of boiling water for 10 minutes. Drain thoroughly.

2 Melt the butter in a large, heavy-based frying skillet and add the red onion wedges, garlic and lemon juice. Cook, stirring constantly for 2–3 minutes.

3 Add the potatoes to the pan and mix well to coat in the butter mixture.

4 Reduce the heat, cover and cook for 25–30 minutes, or until the potatoes are golden brown and tender.

5 Sprinkle the chopped thyme over the top of the potatoes and season.

6 Transfer to a warm serving dish and serve immediately.

2   3   5

main meals

This fabulous collection of mouthwatering recipes is clear proof

that you can eat well without spending too much. Whether your

taste is for pasta, pies, casseroles, curries, or baked dishes, you are

sure to find just the right meal for you and the family. Meat, poultry,

fish, and vegetables all play starring roles at reasonable prices.

spaghetti with meat sauce

$$$

- serves 4
- prepared in 1 hour 5 mins
- cooks in 20 mins

1 tbsp olive oil

1 onion, finely chopped

2 garlic cloves, chopped

1 carrot, scraped and chopped

1 stick celery, chopped

1¾ oz/50 g pancetta or streaky
  bacon, diced

12 oz/350 g lean minced beef

14 oz/400 g can chopped tomatoes

2 tsp dried oregano

4 fl oz/125 ml/scant ½ cup red wine

2 tbsp tomato paste

salt and pepper

675 g/1½ lb fresh spaghetti or
  12 oz/350 g dried spaghetti

1 Heat the oil in a large frying skillet. Add the onions and cook for 3 minutes.

2 Add the garlic, carrot, celery and pancetta or bacon and sauté for 3–4 minutes or until just beginning to brown.

3 Add the beef and cook over a high heat for another 3 minutes or until all of the meat is brown.

4 Stir in the tomatoes, oregano and red wine and bring to the boil. Reduce the heat and leave to simmer for about 45 minutes.

5 Stir in the tomato paste and season with salt and pepper.

6 Cook the spaghetti in a pan of boiling water for 8–10 minutes until tender, but still has 'bite'. Drain thoroughly.

7 Transfer the spaghetti to a serving plate and pour over the meat sauce. Toss to mix well and serve hot.

$$$

beef & dumplings

- serves 6
- prepared in 25 mins
- cooks in 2 hours 30 mins

STEW
2 tbsp corn oil
2 large onions, thinly sliced
8 carrots, sliced
4 tbsp all-purpose flour
salt and pepper
2 lb 12 oz/1.25 kg stewing
  steak, cut into cubes
generous 1¾ cups stout
2 tsp brown sugar
2 bay leaves
1 tbsp chopped fresh thyme
HERB DUMPLINGS
generous ¾ cup self-rising flour
pinch of salt
½ cup shredded suet
2 tbsp chopped fresh parsley,
  plus extra to garnish
about 4 tbsp water

1 Preheat the oven to 325°F/160°C. Heat the oil in a flameproof casserole. Add the onions and carrots and cook over low heat, stirring occasionally, for 5 minutes, or until the onions are softened. Meanwhile, place the flour in a plastic bag and season with salt and pepper. Add the stewing steak to the bag, tie the top, and shake well to coat. Do this in batches, if necessary.

2 Remove the vegetables from the casserole with a perforated spoon and reserve. Add the stewing steak to the casserole, in batches, and cook, stirring frequently, until browned all over. Return all the meat and the onions and carrots to the casserole and sprinkle in any remaining seasoned flour. Pour in the stout and add the sugar, bay leaves, and thyme. Bring to a boil, cover, and transfer to the preheated oven to bake for 1³/₄ hours.

3 To make the herb dumplings, sift the flour and salt into a bowl. Stir in the suet and parsley and add enough of the water to make a soft dough. Shape into role and return to the oven for 30 minutes. Remove and discard the bay leaves and serve, sprinkled with parsley.

1   2   3

beef & tomato gratin

$$

- serves 4
- prepared in 10 mins
- cooks in 1 hour 15 mins

1½ cups lean ground beef
1 large onion, finely chopped
1 tsp dried mixed herbs
1 tbsp all-purpose flour
1¼ cups beef stock
1 tbsp tomato paste
salt and pepper

2 large tomatoes, thinly
  sliced
4 zucchini, thinly sliced
2 tbsp cornstarch
1¼ cups skim milk
⅔ cup mascarpone cheese
1 egg yolk

⅝ cup freshly grated
  Parmesan cheese
crusty bread and
steamed vegetables,
  to serve

1 Preheat the oven to 375°F/190°C. In a large, heavy-bottom skillet, dry-fry the beef and onion over low heat, stirring frequently, for 4–5 minutes, or until the meat is browned all over. Stir in the dried mixed herbs, flour, beef stock, and tomato paste and season to taste with salt and pepper. Bring to a boil, lower the heat, and let simmer gently for 30 minutes, or until the mixture has thickened.

2 Transfer the mixture to an ovenproof gratin dish. Cover with a layer of the sliced tomatoes, then add a layer of sliced zucchinis. Blend the cornstarch with a little milk to make a smooth paste. Pour the remaining milk into a pan and bring to a boil. Add the cornstarch mixture and cook, stirring, for 1–2 minutes, or until thickened. Remove from the heat and beat in the mascarpone cheese and egg yolk. Season to taste with salt and pepper.

3 Spread the white sauce over the layer of zucchini. Place the dish on a cookie sheet and sprinkle with grated Parmesan cheese. Bake in the preheated oven for 25–30 minutes, or until the topping is golden brown and bubbling. Serve with crusty bread and steamed vegetables.

NOTE: If you invest in a block of fresh Parmesan it can be stored in the fridge for a long period and thus becomes an economical ingredient.

spaghetti & meatballs

$$

- serves 6
- prepared in 20 mins, + 30 mins chilling
- cooks in 45 mins

1 oz/25 g white bread, crusts removed and torn into pieces
2 tbsp milk
2 cups fresh ground beef
4 tbsp chopped fresh flat-leaf parsley

1 egg
pinch of cayenne pepper
salt and pepper
2 tbsp olive oil
⅔ cup strained tomatoes
7 oz/200 g canned chopped tomatoes

1¾ cups vegetable stock
pinch of sugar
1 lb/450 g dried spaghetti

1 Place the bread in a small bowl, add the milk and let soak. Meanwhile, place the beef in a large bowl and add half the parsley, the egg, and the cayenne pepper. Season to taste with salt and pepper. Squeeze the excess moisture out of the bread and crumble it over the meat mixture. Mix well until smooth.

1

2 Form small pieces of the mixture into balls between the palms of your hands and place on a baking sheet or board. Let chill in the refrigerator for 30 minutes.

3 Heat the olive oil in a heavy-bottom skillet. Add the meatballs in batches, and cook, stirring and turning frequently, until browned on all sides. Return earlier batches to the skillet, add the strained tomatoes, chopped tomatoes and their can juices, vegetable stock, and sugar, then season to taste with salt and pepper. Bring to a boil, reduce the heat, cover, and let simmer for 25–30 minutes, or until the sauce is thickened and the meatballs are tender and cooked through.

3

4 Meanwhile, bring a large, heavy-bottom pan of lightly salted water to a boil. Add the pasta, return to a boil, and cook for 8–10 minutes, or until tender but still firm to the bite. Drain and transfer to a warmed serving dish. Pour the sauce over the pasta and toss lightly. Sprinkle with the remaining parsley and serve immediately.

4

chili con carne

$$

- serves 4
- prepared in 15 mins
- cooks in 30 - 35 mins

2 tbsp corn oil

1 lb 2 oz/500 g fresh ground beef

1 large onion, chopped

1 garlic clove, finely chopped

1 green bell pepper, seeded and diced

1 tsp chili powder

1 lb 12 oz/800 g canned chopped tomatoes

1 lb 12 oz/800 g canned red kidney beans, drained and rinsed

scant 2 cups beef stock

salt

handful of fresh cilantro sprigs

2 tbsp sour cream, to serve

1 Heat the oil in a large, heavy-bottomed pan or flameproof casserole. Add the beef. Cook over medium heat, stirring frequently, for 5 minutes, or until broken up and browned.

2 Reduce the heat, add the onion, garlic, and bell pepper and cook, stirring frequently, for 10 minutes.

3 Stir in the chili powder, tomatoes and their juices, and kidney beans. Pour in the stock and season with salt. Bring to a boil, reduce the heat and simmer, stirring frequently, for 15–20 minutes, or until the meat is tender.

4 Chop the cilantro sprigs, reserving a few for a garnish, and stir into the chili. Adjust the seasoning, if necessary. Either serve immediately with a splash of sour cream, and cilantro sprigs to garnish, or let cool, then store in the refrigerator overnight. Re-heating the chili the next day makes it more flavorsome.

2   3   4

beef & carrot casserole

$$

- serves 4
- prepared in 10 mins
- cooks in 1 hour 15 mins

1 lb/450 g lean ground beef

1 onion, chopped

1 garlic clove, crushed

1 tbsp all-purpose flour

1 ¼ cups beef bouillon

2 tbsp tomato paste

1 celery stalk, chopped

3 tbsp chopped fresh parsley

1 tbsp Worcestershire sauce

4 cups mealy diced potatoes

2 large carrots, diced

2 tbsp butter

3 tbsp skim milk

salt and pepper

1 Dry-fry the beef in a large pan set over a high heat for 3–4 minutes, or until sealed. Add the onion and garlic and cook for a further 5 minutes, stirring.

2 Add the flour and cook for 1 minute. Gradually blend in the beef bouillon and tomato paste. Stir in the celery, 1 tablespoon of the parsley, and the Worcestershire sauce. Season to taste.

3 Bring the mixture to a boil, then reduce the heat and simmer for 20–25 minutes. Spoon the beef mixture into a 5 cup/1.1 liter pie dish.

4 Meanwhile, cook the potatoes and carrots in a pan of boiling water for 10 minutes. Drain thoroughly and mash them together.

5 Stir the butter, milk, and the remaining parsley into the potato and carrot mixture, and season with salt and pepper to taste. Spoon the potato on top of the beef mixture to cover it completely; alternatively, pipe the potato on top with a pastry bag.

6 Cook the carrot-topped beef pie in a preheated oven, 375°F/190°C, for 45 minutes or until cooked through. Serve piping hot.

$$

meat & potato pot pie

- serves 4 - 5
- prepared in 10 mins
- cooks in 1½ hours

1 lb 9 oz/700 g lean ground lamb
2 onions, chopped
8 oz/225 g carrots, diced
1–2 garlic cloves, crushed
1 tbsp all-purpose flour
7 fl oz/200 ml/ scant 1 cup beef
  stock
7 oz/200 g can chopped
  tomatoes
1 tsp Worcestershire sauce
1 tsp chopped fresh sage or
  oregano or ½ tsp dried sage
  or oregano
750 g–1 kg/1½–2 lb potatoes
1 oz/2/25 g tbsp margarine
3–4 tbsp skimmed milk
125 g/4½ oz button mushrooms,
  optional
salt and pepper

1 Place the meat in a heavy-based saucepan with no extra fat and cook gently, stirring frequently, until the meat begins to brown.

2 Add the onions, carrots and garlic and continue to cook gently for about 10 minutes. Stir in the flour and cook for a minute or so, then gradually stir in the stock and tomatoes and bring to the boil.

3 Add the Worcestershire sauce, seasoning and herbs, cover the pan and simmer gently for about 25 minutes, giving an occasional stir.

4 Cook the potatoes in boiling salted water until tender, then drain thoroughly and mash, beating in the margarine, seasoning and sufficient milk to give a piping consistency. Place in a piping bag fitted with a large star tip.

5 Stir the mushrooms into the meat, if using, and adjust the seasoning.

6 Pipe the potatoes evenly over the meat. Cook in a preheated oven at 400°F/200°C/ for about 30 minutes until piping hot and the potatoes are golden brown.

2

3

5

lamb & vegetable casserole

$$$

- serves 4
- prepared in 45 mins
- cooks in 1¼ hours

1 large eggplant, sliced	or vegetable stock	150 ml/¼ pint/⅔ cup
1 tbsp olive or vegetable oil	2 tbsp cornstarch	natural yogurt
1 onion, chopped finely	2 tbsp water	2 oz/60 g/½ cup grated
1 garlic clove, crushed	1 lb 2 oz/500 g potatoes,	sharp Cheddar cheese
12 oz/350 g lean ground lamb	parboiled for 10 minutes	salt and pepper
9 oz2/50 g mushrooms, sliced	and sliced	fresh flat-leaf parsley,
15 oz/425 g can chopped	2 eggs	to garnish
tomatoes with herbs	4½ oz/125 g/½ cup soft	green salad, to serve
150 ml/¼ pint/⅔ cup lamb	cheese	

1

1 Lay the eggplant slices on a clean surface and sprinkle liberally with salt, to extract the bitter juices. Leave for 10 minutes then turn the slices over and repeat. Put in a colander, rinse and drain well.

2 Meanwhile, heat the oil in a saucepan and fry the onion and garlic for 3–4 minutes. Add the lamb and mushrooms and cook for 5 minutes, until browned. Stir in the tomatoes and stock, bring to the boil and simmer for 10 minutes. Mix the cornstarch with the water and stir into the pan. Cook, stirring, until thickened.

2

3 Spoon half the mixture into an ovenproof dish. Cover with the eggplant slices, then the remaining lamb mixture. Arrange the sliced potatoes on top.

4 Beat together the eggs, soft cheese, yogurt and seasoning. Pour over the potatoes to cover them completely. Sprinkle with the grated cheese.

4

5 Bake in a preheated oven at 375°F/ 190°C for 45 minutes until the topping is set and golden brown. Garnish with flat-leaf parsley and serve with a green salad.

greek lasagna

$$

- serves 4
- prepared in 15 mins
- cooks in 1 hour 40 mins

1 tbsp olive oil	1¼ cups chicken stock	1¼ cups strained plain
1 onion, chopped	(see page 9)	yogurt
2 garlic cloves, finely	salt and pepper	2 eggs, lightly beaten
chopped	1 tsp ground cinnamon	
2 cups fresh ground lamb	4 oz/115 g dried short-cut	
2 tbsp tomato paste	macaroni	
2 tbsp all-purpose flour	2 beefsteak tomatoes, sliced	

1 Preheat the oven to 375°F/190°C. Heat the olive oil in a large heavy-bottom skillet. Add the onion and garlic and cook over low heat, stirring occasionally, for 5 minutes, or until softened. Add the lamb and cook, breaking it up with a wooden spoon, until browned all over. Add the tomato paste and sprinkle in the flour. Cook, stirring, for 1 minute, then stir in the chicken stock. Season to taste with salt and pepper and stir in the cinnamon. Bring to a boil, reduce the heat, cover, and cook for 25 minutes.

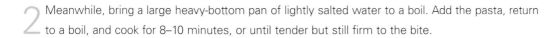

1

2 Meanwhile, bring a large heavy-bottom pan of lightly salted water to a boil. Add the pasta, return to a boil, and cook for 8–10 minutes, or until tender but still firm to the bite.

2

3 Spoon the lamb mixture into a large ovenproof dish and arrange the tomato slices on top. Drain the pasta and transfer to a bowl. Add the yogurt and eggs and mix well. Spoon the pasta mixture on top of the lamb and bake in the preheated oven for 1 hour. Serve immediately.

3

pork with tomato rice

$$

- serves 4
- prepared in 10 mins
- cooks in 55 mins

14 oz/400 g canned chopped
   tomatoes
2½–3 cups beef stock
1 tbsp corn oil
1 lb/450 g fresh ground pork
1 large onion, chopped
1 red bell pepper, seeded and
   chopped
2 cups long-grain rice
1 tbsp chili powder
1 lb/450 g fresh or frozen green
   beans
salt and pepper

1 Preheat the oven to 350°F/ 180°C. Drain the tomatoes, reserving their juices, and reserve. Make the juices up to 3½ cups with the stock and reserve.

2 Heat the oil in a large, flameproof casserole. Add the pork, onion, and red bell pepper and cook over medium heat, stirring frequently, for 8–10 minutes, or until the onion is softened and the meat is broken up and golden brown. Add the rice and cook, stirring constantly, for 2 minutes.

3 Add the tomatoes, stock mixture, chili powder, and beans to the casserole and season to taste with salt and pepper. Bring to a boil, then cover and transfer to the preheated oven to bake for 40 minutes. Serve immediately.

1   2   3

chicken bake

$$

- serves 4
- prepared in 45 mins, +1 hour cooling
- cooks in 40 mins

2¼ cups ground chicken

1 large onion, finely chopped

2 carrots, finely diced

2 tbsp all-purpose flour

1 tbsp tomato paste

1¼ cups chicken stock

salt and pepper

pinch of fresh thyme

2 lb/900 g boiled potatoes,
   creamed with butter and milk
   and highly seasoned

¾ cup grated Jack cheese

freshly cooked peas, to serve

2

1 Dry-fry the ground chicken, onion, and carrots in a large, nonstick pan over low heat, stirring frequently, for 5 minutes, or until the chicken has lost its pink color. Sprinkle the chicken with the flour and cook, stirring constantly, for an additional 2 minutes.

3

2 Gradually blend in the tomato paste and stock, then let simmer for 15 minutes. Season to taste with salt and pepper and add the thyme.

3 Transfer the chicken and vegetable mixture to a large casserole and let cool completely.

4

4 Preheat the oven to 400°F/200°C. Spoon the creamed potato over the chicken mixture and sprinkle with the Jack cheese. Bake in the preheated oven for 20 minutes, or until the cheese is bubbling and golden, then serve with freshly cooked peas.

$$$

chicken with peppers

- serves 4
- prepared in 15 mins
- cooks in 40 mins

8 skinless chicken thighs
2 tbsp whole-wheat flour
2 tbsp olive oil
1 small onion, sliced thinly
1 garlic clove, crushed
1 each large red, yellow and
bell peppers, sliced thinly
14 oz/400 g can chopped
tomatoes
1 tbsp chopped oregano
salt and pepper
fresh oregano, to garnish
crusty whole-wheat bread,
to serve

1 Remove the skin from the chicken thighs and toss in the flour.

2 Heat the oil in a wide frying skillet and fry the chicken quickly until sealed and lightly browned, then remove from the pan.

3 Add the onion to the pan and gently fry until soft. Add the bell peppers, tomatoes and oregano, then bring to the boil, stirring.

4 Arrange the chicken over the vegetables, season well with salt and pepper, then cover the pan tightly and simmer for

20–25 minutes or until the chicken is completely cooked and tender.

5 Season with salt and pepper to taste, garnish with oregano and serve with crusty whole-wheat bread.

1   2   4

jamaican chicken

$$$

- serves 4
- prepared in 5 mins
- cooks in 1¼ hours

2 tsp sunflower oil	2.5 cm/1 inch fresh	garlic salt and cayenne pepper
4 chicken drumsticks	gingerroot, chopped finely	12 oz/350 g corn-on-the-cob
4 chicken thighs	15 oz/425 g can chopped	
1 medium onion	tomatoes	
1 lb 10 oz/750 g piece	½ pint/300 ml/1¼ cups	
squash or pumpkin, peeled	chicken stock	
1 bell pepper	2 oz/60 g/¼ cup split lentils	

2

3

4

1 Heat the oil in a large flameproof casserole and fry the chicken joints, turning frequently, until they are golden all over.

2 Peel and slice the onion.

3 Using a sharp knife, cut the squash or pumpkin into dice.

4 Deseed and slice the bell pepper.

5 Drain any excess fat from the pan and add the onion, pumpkin and pepper. Gently fry for a few minutes. Add the ginger, tomatoes, stock and lentils. Season with garlic salt and cayenne.

6 Cover and place in a preheated oven, 375°F/190°C, for about 1 hour, until the vegetables are tender and the juices from the chicken run clear.

7 Add the drained corn and cook for a further 5 minutes. Season to taste and serve with crusty bread.

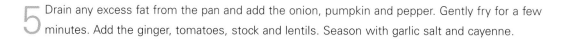

lime chicken

$$

- serves 6
- prepared in 35 mins, + 30 mins marinating
- cooks in 20 mins

3 tbsp finely chopped mint
4 tbsp clear honey
4 tbsp lime juice
12 boneless chicken thighs
salt and pepper
salad, to serve

SAUCE
150 g/5½ oz/½ cup natural
  thick yogurt
1 tbsp finely chopped mint
2 tsp finely grated lime rind

1 Combine the mint, honey and lime juice in a bowl and season with salt and pepper to taste.

2 Use cocktail toothpicks to keep the chicken thighs in neat shapes and add the chicken to the marinade, turning to coat evenly.

3 Leave to the chicken to marinate for at least 30 minutes, longer if possible

4 Cook the chicken on a preheated moderately hot grill or broiler, turning frequently and basting with the marinade.

5 The chicken is cooked if the juices run clear when the chicken is pierced with a skewer.

6 Meanwhile, mix together the sauce ingredients.

7 Remove the cocktail sticks and serve the chicken with a salad and the sauce for dipping or pouring.

1

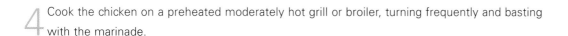

2

6

tuna noodle casserole

$$

- serves 4
- prepared in 20 mins
- cooks in 50 mins

11 oz/300 g dried macaroni

1 tbsp olive oil

1 garlic clove, crushed

2 oz/55 g white mushrooms, sliced

½ red bell pepper, thinly sliced

14 oz/400 g canned tuna in spring water, drained and flaked

1 tsp dried oregano

salt and pepper

SAUCE

2 tbsp butter or margarine, plus extra for greasing

1 tbsp all-purpose flour

1 cup milk

2 tomatoes, sliced

2 tbsp dried bread crumbs

½ cup grated mature Cheddar or Parmesan cheese

1 Preheat the oven to 400°F/ 200°C. Bring a large pan of lightly salted water to a boil. Add the macaroni, return to a boil, and cook for 10–12 minutes, or until tender but still firm to the bite. Drain, rinse, and drain thoroughly.

2 Heat the olive oil in a skillet and cook the garlic, mushrooms, and bell pepper until soft. Add the tuna, oregano, and add salt and pepper to taste. Heat through. Grease a 4-cup/1-liter ovenproof dish with a little butter or margarine. Add half of the cooked macaroni, cover with the tuna mixture, then add the remaining macaroni.

3 To make the sauce, melt the butter or margarine in a pan, stir in the flour and cook for 1 minute. Add the milk gradually and bring to a boil. Simmer for 1–2 minutes, stirring constantly, until thickened. Season to taste with salt and pepper. Pour the sauce over the macaroni. Lay the sliced tomatoes over the sauce and sprinkle with the bread crumbs and cheese. Cook in the preheated oven for 25 minutes, or until piping hot and the top is well browned.

2   3   3

NOTE: If you invest in a block of fresh Parmesan it can be stored in the fridge for a long period and thus becomes an economical ingredient.

smoked fish lasagne

$$$

- serves 4
- prepared in 20 mins
- cooks in 1½ hours

2 tsp olive or vegetable oil

1 garlic clove, crushed

1 small onion, chopped finely

4½ oz mushrooms, sliced

14 oz can chopped tomatoes

1 small zucchini, sliced

⅔ cup vegetable stock or water

2 tbsp butter or margarine

1¼ cups skimmed milk

¼ cup all-purpose flour

1 cup grated sharp Cheddar
  cheese

1 tbsp chopped fresh parsley

4½ oz (6 sheets) pre-cooked
  lasagne

12 oz skinned and boned
  smoked cod or haddock, cut
  into chunks

salt and pepper

fresh parsley sprigs, to garnish

1 Heat the oil in a saucepan and fry the garlic and onion for about 5 minutes. Add the mushrooms and cook for 3 minutes, stirring.

2 Add the tomatoes, zucchini, and stock or water and simmer, uncovered, for 15–20 minutes until the vegetables are soft. Season.

3 Put the butter or margarine, milk, and flour into a small saucepan and heat, whisking constantly, until the sauce boils and thickens. Remove from the heat and add half of the cheese and all of the parsley. Stir gently to melt the cheese and season to taste.

4 Spoon the tomato sauce mixture into a large, shallow baking dish and top with half of the lasagne sheets. Scatter the chunks of fish evenly over the top, then pour over half of the cheese sauce. Top with the remaining lasagne sheets and then spread the rest of the cheese sauce on top. Sprinkle with the remaining cheese.

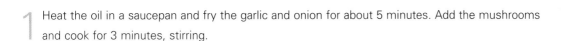

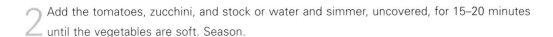

5 Bake in a preheated oven at 375°F for 40 minutes, until the top is golden brown and bubbling. Garnish with parsley sprigs and serve hot.

spaghetti with olives

$$

■ serves 4

■ prepared in 10 mins

■ cooks in 35 - 40 mins

3 tbsp olive oil

2 garlic cloves, finely chopped

10 canned anchovy fillets,
  drained and chopped

scant 1 cup black olives, pitted
  and chopped

1 tbsp capers, drained and rinsed

1 lb/450 g plum tomatoes,
  peeled, seeded, and chopped

pinch of cayenne pepper

salt

14 oz/400 g dried spaghetti

2 tbsp chopped fresh parsley,
  to garnish (optional)

1 Heat the olive oil in a heavy-bottom skillet. Add the garlic and cook over low heat, stirring frequently, for 2 minutes. Add the anchovies and mash them to a pulp with a fork. Add the olives, capers, and tomatoes, and season to taste with cayenne pepper. Cover and let simmer for 25 minutes.

2 Meanwhile, bring a large heavy-bottom pan of lightly salted water to a boil. Add the pasta, return to a boil, and cook for 8–10 minutes, or until tender but still firm to the bite. Drain well and transfer to a warmed serving dish.

3 Spoon the anchovy sauce into the dish and toss the pasta, using 2 large forks. Garnish with the chopped parsley, if using, and serve immediately.

1　　　　　2　　　　　3

tuna spaghetti

$$

- serves 4
- prepared in 20 mins
- cooks in 30 mins

3 tbsp olive oil

4 tomatoes, peeled, seeded, and coarsely chopped

4 oz/115 g mushrooms, sliced

1 tbsp shredded fresh basil

14 oz/400 g canned tuna, drained

generous ⅓ cup fish stock or chicken stock

1 garlic clove, finely chopped

2 tsp chopped fresh marjoram

salt and pepper

12 oz/350 g dried spaghetti

1 cup freshly grated Parmesan cheese, to serve

1

1 Heat the olive oil in a large skillet. Add the tomatoes and cook over low heat, stirring occasionally, for 15 minutes, or until pulpy. Add the mushrooms and cook, stirring occasionally, for an additional 10 minutes. Stir in the basil, tuna, stock, garlic, and marjoram, and season to taste with salt and pepper. Cook over low heat for 5 minutes, or until heated through.

2 Meanwhile, bring a large heavy-bottom pan of lightly salted water to a boil. Add the pasta, return to a boil, and cook for 8–10 minutes, or until tender but still firm to the bite.

1

3 Drain the pasta well, transfer to a warmed serving dish, and spoon on the tuna mixture. Serve with grated Parmesan cheese.

NOTE: If you invest in a block of fresh Parmesan it can be stored in the fridge for a long period and thus becomes an economical ingredient.

2

vegetable curry

$$

- serves 4
- prepared in 5 mins
- cooks in 45 mins

4 tbsp vegetable oil

1 lb 8 oz/675 g waxy
potatoes, cut into
large chunks

2 onions, quartered

3 garlic cloves, crushed

1 tsp garam masala

½ tsp ground turmeric

½ tsp ground cumin

½ tsp ground coriander

2 tsp grated fresh ginger
root

1 fresh red chili, chopped

8 oz/225 g cauliflower
florets

4 tomatoes, peeled and
quartered

¾ cup frozen peas

2 tbsp chopped fresh
cilantro

1¼ cups vegetable stock

shredded fresh cilantro,
to garnish

boiled rice or warm Indian
bread, to serve

1 Heat the vegetable oil in a large heavy pan or skillet. Add the potato chunks, onions, and garlic and fry over low heat, stirring frequently, for 2–3 minutes until the onions are beginning to soften.

2 Add the garam masala, turmeric, ground cumin, ground coriander, ginger, and chili to the pan, mixing the spices into the vegetables until they are well coated. Cook over low heat, stirring constantly, for 1 minute.

1

3 Add the cauliflower, tomatoes, peas, chopped fresh cilantro, and vegetable stock to the curry mixture.

4 Cook the curry over low heat for 30–40 minutes or until the potatoes are tender and completely cooked through.

2

5 Garnish the curry with fresh cilantro and serve with plain boiled rice or warm Indian bread.

3

vegetable enchiladas

$$

- serves 4
- prepared in 20 mins
- cooks in 55 mins

4 flour tortillas
2¾ oz/75 g cup grated
  Cheddar cheese
FILLING
2¾ oz/75 g spinach
2 tbsp olive oil
8 baby corn cobs, sliced
1 tbsp/1 oz/25 g frozen peas,
  thawed
1 bell pepper, seeded and diced
1 carrot, diced
1 leek, sliced
2 garlic cloves, crushed
1 red chili, chopped
salt and pepper
SAUCE
300 ml/½ pint/1¼ cups sieved
  tomatoes
2 shallots, chopped
1 garlic clove, crushed
300 ml/½ pint/1¼ cups
  vegetable stock
1 tsp superfine sugar
1 tsp chili powder

1 To make the filling, blanch the spinach in a pan of boiling water for 2 minutes. Drain well, pressing out as much excess moisture as possible, and chop.

2 Heat the oil in a frying skillet over a medium heat. Add the baby corn cobs, bell pepper, carrot, leek, garlic and chili and sauté, stirring briskly, for 3–4 minutes. Stir in the spinach and season well with salt and pepper to taste.

3 Put all the sauce ingredients in a heavy-based saucepan and bring to the boil, stirring constantly. Cook over a high heat, stirring constantly, for 20 minutes, until thickened and reduced by a third.

4 Spoon a quarter of the filling along the centre of each tortilla. Roll the tortillas around the filling and place, seam side down, in a single layer in an ovenproof dish.

5 Pour the sauce over the tortillas and sprinkle the cheese on top. Cook in a preheated oven, 350°F/180°C for 20 minutes, or until the cheese has melted and browned. Serve immediately.

2   4   4

hearty stew

$

- serves 4
- prepared in 20 mins
- cooks in 30 mins

3 tbsp olive oil
1 onion, sliced
generous 1 cup thinly
   sliced mushrooms
2 garlic cloves, chopped
   very finely
1 tsp dried oregano

2 tbsp tomato paste
3 tbsp chopped fresh
   flat-leaf parsley
1lb 12 oz/800 g canned
   chopped tomatoes
2 cups chicken stock
2 cups dried short macaroni

1 tsp salt
¼ tsp pepper
freshly grated
   Parmesan, to serve

1 Heat the olive oil in a large pan or high-sided skillet with a lid, over medium heat. Add the onion and mushrooms. Cook, stirring frequently, for 5–7 minutes, or until soft.

2 Stir in the garlic, oregano, tomato paste, and 1½ tablespoons of the parsley. Cook for 1 minute. Pour in the tomatoes and stock. Bring to a boil.

3 Add the macaroni, salt, and pepper. Bring back to a boil. Cover and simmer over medium–low heat for 20 minutes, stirring occasionally, or until the macaroni is tender.

4 Sprinkle with the remaining parsley just before serving. Serve with freshly grated Parmesan.

NOTE: If you invest in a block of fresh Parmesan it can be stored in the fridge for a long period and thus becomes an economical ingredient

cold weather casserole

$$

- serves 6
- prepared in 20 mins
- cooks in 1 hour 15 mins

¼ cup butter or
   vegetarian margarine
2 leeks, sliced
2 carrots, sliced
2 potatoes, cut into bite-size
   pieces
1 rutabaga, cut into bite-size
   pieces
2 zucchini, sliced
1 fennel bulb, halved and sliced
2 tbsp all-purpose flour
15 oz/425 g canned lima beans
2½ cups vegetable stock
2 tbsp tomato paste
1 tsp dried thyme
2 bay leaves
salt and pepper
DUMPLINGS
generous ¾ cup self-rising flour
pinch of salt
½ cup vegetarian suet
2 tbsp chopped fresh parsley
about 4 tbsp water

1 Melt the butter in a large, heavy-bottomed pan over low heat. Add the leeks, carrots, potatoes, rutabaga, zucchini, and fennel and cook, stirring occasionally, for 10 minutes. Stir in the flour and cook, stirring constantly, for 1 minute. Stir in the can juice from the beans, the stock, tomato paste, thyme, and bay leaves and season to taste with salt and pepper. Bring to a boil, stirring constantly, then cover and simmer for 10 minutes.

2 Meanwhile, make the dumplings. Sift the flour and salt into a bowl. Stir in the suet and parsley, then add enough water to bind to a soft dough. Divide the dough into 8 pieces and roll into balls.

3 Add the lima beans and dumplings to the pan, cover, and simmer for an additional 30 minutes. Remove and discard the bay leaf before serving.

1   2   3

mushroom & bean chili

$

- serves 6
- prepared in 10 mins
- cooks in 50 mins

4 tbsp olive oil
8 oz/225 g small white
  mushrooms
1 large onion, chopped
1 garlic clove, chopped
1 green bell pepper, seeded
  and cut into strips

1 tsp each paprika, ground
  coriander, and ground cumin
¼–½ tsp chili powder
14 oz/400 g canned chopped
  tomatoes
⅔ cup vegetable stock
1 tbsp tomato paste
14 oz/400 g canned red kidney

beans, drained and rinsed
salt and pepper
2 tbsp chopped fresh cilantro

1 Heat 1 tablespoon of the oil in a large skillet. Add the mushrooms and stir-fry until golden. Remove with a slotted spoon and set aside until required.

2 Add the remaining oil to the skillet. Add the onion, garlic, and green bell pepper and cook for 5 minutes. Stir in the paprika, coriander, cumin, and chili powder and cook for an additional 1 minute.

3 Add the tomatoes, stock, and tomato paste, stir well, then cover and let cook for 20 minutes.

4 Add the reserved mushrooms and kidney beans and cook, covered, for an additional 20 minutes. Season to taste with salt and pepper and stir in the cilantro. Serve at once.

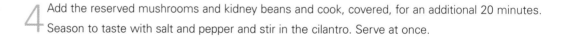

chickpea casserole

- serves 4
- prepared in 15 mins
- cooks in 2 hours 30 mins

8 oz/225 g dried chickpeas, soaked overnight in enough water to cover
3 tbsp olive oil
1 large onion, sliced
2 garlic cloves, finely chopped
2 leeks, sliced
6 oz/175 g carrots, sliced

4 turnips, sliced
4 celery stalks, sliced
4 oz/115 g bulgur wheat
14 oz/400 g canned chopped tomatoes
2 tbsp snipped fresh chives, plus extra to garnish
salt and pepper

1 Drain the chickpeas and place in a heavy-bottomed pan. Add enough water to cover, bring to a boil, and simmer for 1¹/₂ hours.

2 Meanwhile, heat the oil in a large pan. Add the sliced onion and cook, stirring, for 5 minutes, or until softened. Add the garlic, leeks, carrots, turnips, and celery and cook, stirring occasionally, for 5 minutes. Stir in the bulgur wheat, tomatoes, and chives, season to taste with salt and pepper, and bring to a boil. Spoon the mixture into a heatproof pudding bowl, cover with a lid of foil, and reserve.

1

3 When the chickpeas have been cooking for 1¹/₂ hours, set a steamer over the pan. Place the basin inside the steamer, cover tightly, and cook for an additional 40 minutes. Remove the basin from the steamer, drain the chickpeas, then stir them into the vegetable and bulgur wheat mixture. Transfer to a warmed serving dish and serve immediately, garnished with extra chives.

2

3

vegetable casserole

$

- serves 4
- prepared in 15 mins
- cooks in 40 mins

1 cauliflower, cut into florets
salt and pepper
2 tbsp corn oil
2½ tbsp all-purpose flour
1½ cups milk
1½ oz/325 g canned corn
   kernels, drained
2 tbsp chopped fresh parsley
1 tsp chopped fresh thyme
scant 1½ cups grated Cheddar
   cheese
TOPPING
6 tbsp whole-wheat flour
2 tbsp butter
½ cup rolled oats
⅛ cup blanched almonds,
   chopped

1 Preheat the oven to 375°F/190°C. Cook the cauliflower in a pan of lightly salted boiling water for 5 minutes. Drain well, reserving the cooking water. Heat the oil in a pan and stir in the flour. Cook, stirring constantly, for 1 minute. Remove the pan from the heat and gradually stir in the milk and ²/₃ cup of the reserved cooking water. Return the pan to the heat and bring to a boil, stirring constantly. Cook, stirring, for 3 minutes, or until thickened. Remove the pan from the heat.

2 Stir the corn, parsley, thyme, and half the cheese into the sauce and season to taste with salt and pepper. Fold in the cauliflower, then spoon the mixture into an ovenproof dish.

3 To make the crumble topping, place the flour in a bowl, add the butter, and rub it in with your fingertips until the mixture resembles bread crumbs. Stir in the oats and almonds, add the remaining cheese, then sprinkle the mixture evenly over the vegetables. Bake in the preheated oven for 30 minutes, then serve.

1   2   3

vegetable & lentil casserole

$

- serves 4
- prepared in 15 mins
- cooks in 2 hours

1 onion	2 carrots, chopped
4 cloves	3 zucchini, sliced
1⅓ cups Puy or green lentils	1 celery stick, chopped
1 bay leaf	1 red bell pepper, seeded and
6–7 cups vegetable bouillon or	chopped
water	1 tbsp lemon juice
2 leeks, sliced	salt and ground black pepper
2 potatoes, diced	

1 Spike the onion with the cloves. Put the lentils in a large casserole, add the onion and bay leaf, and pour in the vegetable bouillon or water. Cover and bake in a preheated oven, 350°F/180°C, for 1 hour.

2 Remove the casserole from the oven. Take out the onion and discard the cloves. Slice the onion and return it to the casserole with the leeks, potatoes, carrots, zucchini, celery, and red bell pepper.

3 Stir thoroughly and season to taste with salt and pepper. Cover and return to the oven for a further hour.

4 Discard the bay leaf. Stir the lemon juice into the casserole and serve it immediately on warmed serving plates.

1

1

2

desserts

Forget over-processed, costly, and unsatisfying pots of yogurt and frozen desserts and rediscover traditional and economical favorites such as Chocolate Cake with Hot Fudge Sauce, Apple Pie, and Fruit Brûlée. You'll notice the difference in the smiles on the family's faces and the extra change in your purse.

chocolate cake with hot fudge sauce

$$

- serves 6
- prepared in 10 mins
- cooks in 35 - 40 mins

generous ⅓ cup soft margarine

1¼ cups self-rising flour

½ cup light corn syrup

3 eggs

¼ cup unsweetened cocoa

CHOCOLATE FUDGE SAUCE

3½ oz/100 g dark chocolate

½ cup sweetened condensed
   milk

4 tbsp heavy cream

1 Lightly grease a 5 cup/1.2 liter heatproof bowl.

2 Place the ingredients for the sponge in a separate mixing bowl and beat until well combined and smooth.

3 Spoon into the prepared bowl and level the top. Cover with a disk of waxed paper and tie a pleated sheet of aluminum foil over the bowl. Steam for 1½-2 hours until the sponge is cooked and springy to the touch.

4 To make the sauce, break the chocolate into small pieces and place in a small pan with the sweetened condensed milk. Heat gently, stirring, until the chocolate has melted.

5 Remove the pan from the heat and stir in the heavy cream.

6 To serve the dessert, turn it out onto a warm serving plate and pour over a little of the chocolate fudge sauce. Serve immediately, handing round the remaining sauce separately.

2

3

5

orange meringue custard

- serves 8
- prepared in 15 mins, +15 mins standing
- cooks in 50 mins

2 tbsp butter, plus extra for
  greasing
2½ cups milk
generous 1 cup superfine
  sugar
finely grated rind of
  1 orange
4 eggs, separated

1⅜ cups fresh bread crumbs
salt
6 tbsp orange marmalade

1 Grease a 6-cup/1.5-liter ovenproof dish with butter.

2 To make the custard, heat the milk in a pan with the butter, ¼ cup of the superfine sugar, and the grated orange rind until just warm.

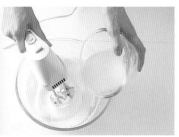

3 Whisk the egg yolks in a bowl. Gradually pour the warm milk over the eggs, whisking constantly. Stir the bread crumbs into the bowl, then transfer the mixture to the dish and let stand for 15 minutes.

4 Preheat the oven to 350°F/180°C, then bake the pudding for 20–25 minutes, until the custard has just set. Remove the custard from the oven, but do not turn the oven off.

5 To make the meringue, whisk the egg whites with a pinch of salt in a spotlessly clean, greasefree bowl until soft peaks form. Whisk in the remaining sugar, a little at a time. Spread the orange marmalade over the cooked custard. Top with the meringue, spreading it right to the edges of the dish. Return the pudding to the oven and bake for an additional 20 minutes, or until the meringue is crisp and golden.

bread & butter pudding

$

- serves 4
- prepared in 15 mins
- cooks in 40

6 medium slices of day-old
  whole-wheat bread, crusts
  removed
2 tbsp butter
2 tbsp sugar
1 tbsp golden raisins
1½ tbsp currants
generous 1¾ cups milk

2 eggs
½ tsp ground allspice

1 Preheat the oven to 350°F/180°C. Spread the slices of bread with butter, then cut each slice into fourths. Arrange half of the bread, buttered side up, on the bottom of a 3½-cup ovenproof dish. Sprinkle over half of the sugar, then scatter over half of the golden raisins and currants. Top with the remaining bread, then sprinkle over the remaining sugar and fruit.

2 Pour the milk into a large mixing bowl. Add the eggs and allspice and whisk until smooth. Pour the mixture evenly over the bread, then transfer to the preheated oven and bake for about 40 minutes. Remove from the oven and serve hot.

1

1

1

apple pie

$$

- serves 6
- prepared in 50 mins
- cooks in 55 mins

1¾–2¼ lb cooking apples,
   peeled, cored, and sliced
scant ¾ cup brown or white
   sugar, plus extra for sprinkling
½–1 tsp ground cinnamon, apple
   spice, or ground ginger
1–2 tbsp water
SHORTCRUST PIE DOUGH
3 cups all-purpose flour
pinch of salt
6 tbsp butter or margarine
6 tbsp white vegetable
   shortening
about 6 tbsp cold water
beaten egg or milk, for glazing

1 To make the pie dough, sift the flour and salt into a mixing bowl. Add the butter or margarine and shortening and rub in with the fingertips until the mixture resembles fine bread crumbs. Add the water and gather the mixture together into a dough. Wrap the dough in foil and chill for 30 minutes.

2 Roll out almost two-thirds of the pie dough thinly and use it to line an 8–9 inch/20–23 cm deep pie plate or shallow pie pan.

3 Mix the apples with the sugar and spice and pack into the pie shell; the filling can come up above the rim. Add the water if liked, particularly if the apples are a dry variety.

4 Roll out the remaining pie dough to form a lid. Dampen the edges of the pie rim with water and position the lid, pressing the edges firmly together. Trim the edges and crimp them decoratively.

5 Use the trimmings to cut out leaves or other shapes to decorate the top of the pie, dampen, and attach. Glaze the top of the pie with beaten egg or milk, make 1–2 slits in the top, and put the pie on a cookie sheet.

6 Bake the pie in a preheated oven, 425°F/220°C, for 20 minutes, then reduce the temperature to 350°F/180°C and cook for a further 30 minutes, or until the pastry is a light golden brown. Serve the pie hot or cold, sprinkled with brown or white sugar.

3   4   5

fruit brûlée

$$

- serves 4
- prepared in 15 mins
- cooks in 1¼ hour

4 plums, pitted and sliced
2 cooking apples, peeled and
   sliced
1 tsp ground ginger
600 ml/1 pint/2½ cups Greek-
   style yogurt
2 tbsp confectioner's sugar,
   sifted

1 tsp almond extract
2¾ oz/75 g/⅓ cup brown crystal
   sugar

2

1 Put the plums and apples in a saucepan with 2 tablespoons of water and cook for 7–10 minutes, until tender, but not mushy. Set aside to cool, then stir in the ginger.

2 Using a slotted spoon, spoon the mixture into the base of a shallow serving dish.

3

3 Mix the yogurt, confectioner's sugar and almond extract and spoon on to the fruit to cover.

4 Sprinkle the brown crystal sugar over the top of the yogurt and cook under a hot broiler for 3–4 minutes, or until the sugar has dissolved and formed a crust.

5 Leave to chill in the refrigerator for 1 hour and serve.

4

lemon meringue pie

$$

- serves 4
- prepared in 20 minutes, + 30 minutes to rest
- cooks in 1 hour

PIE DOUGH

scant 1½ cups all-purpose flour,
  plus extra for dusting

scant ½ cup butter, diced, plus
  extra for greasing

scant ½ cup confectioner's
  sugar, sifted

finely grated zest of 1 lemon

1 egg yolk, beaten

3 tbsp milk

FILLING

3 tbsp cornstarch

1¼ cups cold water

juice and grated zest of 2
  lemons

scant 1 cup superfine sugar

2 eggs, separated

1 To make the pie dough, sift the flour into a bowl and rub in the butter. Mix in the remaining ingredients. Knead briefly on a lightly floured counter. Let rest for 30 minutes. Preheat the oven to 350°F/180°C. Grease an 8-inch/20-cm ovenproof pie dish with butter. Roll out the dough to a thickness of ¼ inch/5 mm and use it to line the dish. Prick with a fork, line with baking parchment, and fill with baking beans. Bake for 15 minutes. Remove from the oven. Lower the temperature to 300°F/150°C.

2 To make the filling, mix the cornstarch with a little water. Put the remaining water into a pan. Stir in the lemon juice and zest and cornstarch paste. Bring to a boil, stirring. Cook for 2 minutes. Cool a little. Stir in 5 tablespoons of sugar and the egg yolks, and pour into the tart shell. In a separate bowl, whisk the egg whites until stiff. Gradually whisk in the remaining sugar and spread over the pie. Bake for 40 minutes. Remove from the oven and serve.

2

2

2

$$

pear cake

- serves 12
- prepared in 25 mins
- cooks in 1½ hours

4 pears, peeled and cored

margarine, for greasing

2 tbsp water

7 oz/200 g/1½ all-purpose
  flour

2 tsp baking powder

3½ oz/100 g/½ cup soft
  light brown sugar

4 tbsp milk

2 tbsp clear honey, plus
  extra to drizzle

2 tsp ground cinnamon

2 egg whites

1 Grease and line the base of a 20 cm/8 inch cake pan.

2 Put 1 pear in a food processor with the water and blend until almost smooth. Transfer to a mixing bowl.

3 Sieve in the all-purpose flour and baking powder. Beat in the sugar, milk, honey and cinnamon and mix well.

3

4 Chop all but one of the remaining pears and add to the mixture.

5 Whisk the egg whites until peaking and gently fold into the mixture until fully blended.

6 Slice the remaining pear and arrange in a fan pattern on the base of the pan.

6

7 Spoon the cake mixture into the pan and cook in a preheated oven, at 300°F/150°C, for 1¼ –1½ hours or until cooked through.

8 Remove the cake from the oven and leave to cool in the pan for 10 minutes.

7

9 Turn the cake out on to a wire cooling rack and drizzle with honey. Leave to cool completely, then cut into slices to serve.

chocolate fruit crumble

$$$

- serves 4
- prepared in 10 mins
- cooks in 40 - 45 mins

6 tbsp butter, plus extra for
   greasing
14 oz/400 g canned apricots,
   in natural juice
1 lb/450 g cooking apples,
   peeled and thickly sliced
scant ⅔ cup all-purpose flour
½ cup rolled oats

4 tbsp superfine sugar
generous ½ cup chocolate
   chips

1 Preheat the oven to 180°C/350°F. Grease an ovenproof dish with a little butter.

2 Drain the apricots, reserving 4 tablespoons of the juice. Place the apples and apricots in the prepared ovenproof dish with the reserved apricot juice and toss to mix thoroughly.

2

3 Sift the flour into a large bowl. Cut the butter into small cubes and rub it in with your fingertips until the mixture resembles fine bread crumbs. Stir in the rolled oats, superfine sugar, and chocolate chips.

3

4 Sprinkle the crumble mixture over the apples and apricots and level the top roughly. Do not press the crumble down onto the fruit. Bake in the preheated oven for 40–45 minutes, or until the topping is golden. Serve the crumble hot or cold.

4

index